I'm Praying for You Always…
The Anomalous Life of an Intercessor

By L.S. Reed

Nashville TN

First Printing: 2015

ISBN 978-1-943616-00-8

MAWMedia Group, LLC
2525 Somerset Drive
Nashville, TN 37217

www.mawmedia.com

Cover photo by T. Lee Ellison

DEDICATION

This book is dedicated to the memory of one of my spiritual mother, **Sis. Lillie Tynes**, whose, Prayer Ministry touched me in a very personal way and spanned numerous decades to reach many people around the globe and especially those who knew and loved her in the greater metro- Denver, Colorado area.

ACKNOWLEDGEMENTS

To God, my heavenly Father, I give praise and honor for the privilege to share Your love for me with others. To both of my sons Juan and Michael, for always believing in me. I love you. To each of my fellow Prayer Warriors, for the tons of prayers and encouragement you have given, thank you. To the host of gifted and talented folk who assisted me in the nuts and bolts of getting published, I am eternally grateful.

Table of Contents

Foreword

The writer is truly blessed with a love relationship with God her heavenly Father. Just as Enoch began his walk with God, she too is walking in a light that comes from the great love of Jesus. She forwards the idea that Jesus teaches us that we should trust God. This book suggests to the readers that prayer is a sort of verbal intercourse with God which sustains us through every trial and hurt. The writer makes the case that even through the loss of our children we can still be drawn closer to God. Throughout the book the readers are given a real glimpse into suffering similar to that of Job and what it looks like to believe solely in the righteousness of Christ.

The trying times that the writer has gone through and survived shine a light of hope for anyone who experiences loss and the fallout of broken relationships. While she has struggles in her own life, with God she manages to rise above her circumstances and is not defeated by them. With the combination of faith in God and much prayer the writer continues her walk with God. In the midst of her storms she supports the idea that with God we are never really alone.

The writer maintains a position that everyone at some point in life's journey will face some kind of trial or temptations. But she demonstrates by example how they can serve to develop character and leave us stronger with the right attitude. She is equally thorough in her assertions about the challenges that are inherent in life and that no one is left out of the equation when it comes to problems. Her opinion is that if you don't see it now; just keep on living! And that where there is no test there is no testimony.

The poetic, intuitive words of wisdom and inspiring stories in this book leaves the readers with hope for tomorrow and sheer joy in the moment. At times the writer captivates us with riveting unveilings of God's hand of mercy as it were reaching out from heaven to deliver her from the sting of death. She tastefully guides us into the awesome domain of Intercessory prayer with the conviction that God is pleading and searching for those who are willing to stand in the gap for souls. After reading this book you the readers will be persuaded that God is willing and able to answer our prayers; God answers sometimes even before we call. And you will be blessed with an inundated understanding of how the Holy Spirit assumes a vital part in our prayers.

This book is about one mother's pervasive look as it were into the face of Jesus, with resolve that would not succumb to doubt nor fear and the audacity to believe that with a child-like faith in God and sincere prayers to Him everything would be alright. You the readers will be held spellbound from cover to cover. Enjoy!!

Trish Nealey, Fomer Prayer Warrior Leader
Park Hill SDA Church, Denver, CO.

Introduction

Have you ever been in situations where you couldn't do nothing but pray? It has been like that for me non-stop it seems. I believe prayer is more of God calling us into intimacy with Him rather than us beating down His door to get with Him. There are times I simply do not feel like praying. I believe I can be honest about it because, God knows all about me and He loves me anyhow. I'm just keeping it real.

For all those reading this, God loves you too. This book came about in response to God nudging me to be at-one with Him. These days it doesn't take much to get me distracted from my time with God. Every morning I wake up it feels like a set-up from God to get my attention. So now He has it. And I am answering His call to write this book about one of the abiding things that has kept me thus far, PRAYER.

As a little girl I sensed God in my life when I didn't even know there was a God. I could feel His warmth and love when I did not feel loved or lovely. It was that childlike trust in a presence I had no identity for. I just know that it sought me out and drew me in like nothing else I have ever known could. It was so easy for me to fall in love with this God and Jesus as a child. My first memory of praying to God was as a naive nine year old girl. My father had taken ill and it broke my heart.

I prayed for my Daddy to get well. Daddy got better and from that moment forward I began my journey with God via prayer. The journey has been everything I have ever desired or wanted and more. I carried my prayer alter with me while serving in the Military. As a young married woman I erected a family alter of prayer. As I matriculated through the schools of Higher Learning my prayer alter was with me.

During my Pastoral formation and Chaplain Internship prayer was my stay. As a Missionary in South Korea prayer was at the heart and forefront of that experience. All throughout my Christian walk, while wearing many hats in the gospel ministry, and as a worshipper of God, He has called me to prayer.

I will take you on a journey into the various venues in which I have experienced an anointed and appointed prayer life. The life of an intercessor is a special calling and should be entered into knowing that God is in it to win it. His call and gifts are without repentance. It is the work of a lifetime.

At the end of each topic is a five-day exercise to complete. The exercise is designed to tantalize and stimulate your memory. You will also gain invaluable information when you complete the exercises that you can apply to your own spiritual journey as a Christian or Intercessor. So it is with much joy and a heart that is grateful to God that I share with you the personal experiences, insights and vision God has given me as an Intercessor about Prayer!

GOD HAS SPOKEN

From the depths of His uttermost, God has spoken
Through the tomb of my nothingness

God has spoken
From the pinnacle of His omnipotence God has spoken
Through the fleeting of my consciousness

God has spoken
From the breadth of His holiness God has spoken
Through the shame of my sinfulness

God has spoken
From the gift of His selflessness God has spoken
Through the mending of my brokenness

God has spoken
From the grace of His peacefulness God has spoken
Through the yearning of my restlessness

God has spoken

By LS Reed

Chapter 1

A SOLDIER'S SALUTE TO PRAYER

"Uncle Sam Wants You". I had no idea that commercial was even remotely referring to me. I was nearing the end of my boring experience of High School. I was barely getting by, with my academic performance. I felt back then that my parents hated me. I was a prisoner on house arrest; at least it felt like that. I didn't have an ankle bracelet but the restrictions placed on me by my parents didn't allow for much freedom either.

I really wasn't too concerned that I was ranked at the bottom third of my graduating class that year. I just wanted it to be over!! The year was 1963. Your experience may have been a lot different from mine. But do you recall what it was like? You may find we have more in common than you think. Here is what my past High school days were like.

The heat of summer was already evident in the ninety plus degree temperatures. As sweat trickled down my back underneath my bargain basement blouse (I had purchased with my lunch money that was on sale at Zablosky's), I day dreamed about life away from the demands of School and my parents. I really had no real plans at all. During that time in my life I remember just wanting things to be different and better for me.

I had it as good as most back then. My daddy worked hard and we had a roof over our heads and food and all. But I wanted more.

The problem was, I had no clue what it was like to have more. My life was ordinary and it seemed to be lacking in luster, with added no frills, and no adventure or excitement in it.

Every day of my boring existence as a high School teen was pretty much predictable. On school days I was up by 6:00 a.m. I swallowed down without really taking the time to chew very much, a quick bowl of cereal. Racing across the dull lacquer on the kitchen floor, I would with precision quickly grab my blouse and skirt from off the drying rack.

I often ended up washing them by hand the night before. Next I would continue my routine of setting up the ironing board, sprinkling my outfit with water to get the wrinkles out, iron my outfit. The rest of my routine was like a windup toy on automatic pilot. I would with haste do a quick hand wash of my body, brush my teeth, jump into my outfit, comb and style my hair, put on my make-up and dash out the door for the bus stop three blocks down from our house on Martindale.

Make-up for women of color back then came in only a few shades. If you happened to be a shade off you got stuck with a shade that did not really compliment your true skin color. I wore a shade that did not match very well. My brother Roy was always telling me I had on too much make-up. I would look in the mirror in our dimly lit bathroom and see me as a beautiful cover girl for a magazine and wonder what all his fuss was about. Going by what I know about make-up these days and comparing now to how I wore make-up back then in the sixties is hilarious. I understand what Roy must have seen on my face (a weird color face powder in patches, ugly Red color cheek rouge that would make a clown blush, and lips way too red).

Back then finding clothes to wear to school was about as easy as threading a needle blindfolded with a glove on. I had no older sisters living with me growing up to provide me with hand me downs. So there may have been some slight variations in my daily routine. It varied depending on the available clothes I had to work with or washed in the washer the weekend before that school week. Or it was simply how late I was running time wise that morning. Most of the time, I was rushed because I overslept.

I didn't get much sleep most nights. I always heard weird, strange sounds in the house at night. The stairs creaked and I swear I could hear whispers and things moving and falling or knocking around in the rooms of our house. Day or night, it didn't matter, our rickety old house felt haunted to me. There were even stories of ghost sighted in our house by the family that lived there prior to our moving in.

Then there was the fact that I was always the brunt of my momma's nagging, whenever I rushed to get ready. She began nagging from the time I came downstairs, and she didn't let up until my feet hit the sidewalk running for the bus stop. I ran every morning late or not, hail, rain, sleet or snow, just to get away from momma's nagging.

The summer was unbearably hot and sulky in Indianapolis as time rolled on. My school days were almost over and my time would be mine at last. I would be graduating with the Class of 1963.

Graduating from High School, was supposed to be a landmark of achievement back then. I almost didn't graduate because of my own doing. I had my own version of chasing my blues away back then, it was known as cutting classes. I was an expert at it. I simply cut the classes that I didn't like, but I attend school every day.

I almost got away with it. I was found out when a review of my academic progress was made by the academic board that determined who was ready for graduation. It turned out that I had just enough credits to graduate with a "General" Diploma. That was a blow to me because I was placed in the advanced track of studies when I started my high school studies, and it offered the kind of degree that would best prepare me for nursing school once I graduated.

As if that disappointment wasn't bad enough, my momma had to come to the high school to talk to the school counselor to sign off on the offer to graduate with a "General" diploma. During that meeting I expressed my disdain for my whole existence as a human being, which included the fact that I was still a virgin. Getting back to more pleasantries I fluffed up my bangs and leaned back in my rocking chair and thought about what it might be like to go to college like my older brother Carl. It was only a brief flight of ideas of course.

College had not been one of my options. It was an option reserved for males only in our family. So, my best option was to get a job and move out on my own. There was a problem with that option. I had never worked a real job a day in my life, just babysitting. Then there was daddy's doting suggestion that I could get married. I almost passed out at the thought of it. Married to whom? I had never even been engaged. I did have a boyfriend at the time, but we had just started dating my last year of high school. We barely knew each other and even less about getting married. I was seventeen and my boyfriend was only fifteen at the time.

Thank God for sisters. My older sister Juanita offered to take me to Detroit with her that summer after I graduated. That seemed tempting to me. Maybe I could find work there. At least there I would be a way from my boring existence living at home with my parents. So when I graduated High School, my sister and I left for Detroit.

The summer of 1963 remained hot and sulky. After only two days in Detroit I realized it was not the place for me. I was actually terrified at the thought of living there. I heard loud gun shots at night and my Uncle had so many locks on his doors I thought I was at Ft. Knox. To make matters worse, a man had been murdered just a few doors down from where we were staying. When my sister announced that she was ready to go back home to Indianapolis I was happy to be going back there with her.

When we got back to my house, home never looked better to me. But as the summer passed on I was soon thrust into in panic mode. What if I never get out of my parents' house, or never get a job, or never get married?

I was at my wits end when my buddy, Alfrieda, came up with what I thought was a brilliant idea at the time. It would solve my job problem. I would be out of my parent's hose. I could travel to faraway places and see the world. I could even work hard and maybe even graduate top of my training class.

The plan was that she and I would join the Army together on the buddy plan. That way, we could do basic training at the same military base, and possibly be stationed together. So we contacted a recruiter and our plan began to unfold.

The recruiter began to prep me for the written exam and instructed me to eat as much as possible to bring my weight up to regulation standards. I was about thirty-five pounds underweight at that time. So I began to stuff myself with extra helpings and all the foods that would put on the pounds. At weigh-in time I was still about fifteen pounds off, but I was cleared on my physical anyhow. I signed up for three years to secure my placement choice in the Medical Corps.

The year was still 1963. It was now October, my birth month. I had little or no contact with Alfrieda during this time. I stayed pretty much focused on getting myself ready to be sworn into the Army. I passed the written exams and surprisingly scored fairly high on the mechanical concept exam questions.

It was a few days away from my eighteenth birthday that it began to sink in that I was actually going to be leaving home. Not only that, I was going to fly for the very first time in my life and be among complete strangers, in a city I had never been to. I comforted myself with the fact that Alfrieda, was going with me. At least I thought so at the time.

The sun came up over the horizon like any other day in October. I pulled the covers from off my face and peered out around my bedroom. I was taking in the symmetrical designs in the flowery wall paper on the walls. I let my eyes focus on the half pulled window shade and noticed a tiny bird perched on the seal just outside my window. The sun's warmth felt deliciously soothing.

Beams of sunlight shown across my bed onto the floor in front of my bed. I wiped the sleep from my eyes and stretched my body briefly while turning and placing my feet firmly on the woven rug on the floor. Today was the day I was to say yes to Uncle Sam. It was October 29, 1963. I tried to imagine what it would be like at the swearing in ceremony. Maybe that word is too formal. It's not like I'm a Politian or something. Actually I am an unknown, except Uncle Sam wants me. I wondered for a moment what Alfrieda was doing. I just realized we had not been in contact with each other for weeks now.

My mind drifted back to my room. My mind went back to when my parents first fixed this room up girly style just for me. I was twelve at the time. They thought it would be improper for me to sleep in the same room with my brothers coming into womanhood. My menstrual hadn't begun yet so I didn't know what all the fuss was about. In fact I was a late bloomer. I was actually sixteen when my menstrual started. This room had served me well. I felt a warm glow on the inside as my eyes swept around my room once more.

I was jolted back into more sobering thoughts by momma's voice shouting up the stairs at me. The recruiter had called to say he was on the way to pick me up to take me to the Recruitment station. I scrambled to get ready. It seemed my recruiter was here in a flash. I was finally on my way to get married to Uncle Sam…

I came back home after being sworn into the Army in a daze. The thoughts inside of my head seemed to move in slow motion and my heart started pounding in my chest like a drum. What in heaven's name had I just done? It was at that moment I really and truly began to feel an enormous sense of aloneness. I was no longer an unknown anymore. I had stood with other men and women, strangers I didn't know and took an oath to serve in a military I knew even less about.

A whole new world would be opening up to me and I felt the mystery of it all pulling me, drawing me towards it, like a dark giant cesspool of unknowns. To my dismay my buddy and comrade, Alfrieda, had not even showed up there at the station to be sworn in! She had changed her mind of course and conveniently forgot to share that bit of news with me. I felt abandoned and betrayed. It was at that moment I also began to sense God drawing me into His arms. His familiar, soothing warmth was in the room with me. It was so easy to welcome God's call to prayer, to be at one with Him, and to be comforted by Him.

I had no spoken request to God, only a heart wrenching desperate plea for help deep within. Only God could relieve that twisted gnawing fear I felt inside. I was leaving everything and everyone I had known, and the safety and shelter of my parent's house. I had not even left home yet and already I had a foreboding sense of danger ahead, and a pocket full of regrets.

I had very little time left to say my good- byes. I broke the news to my boyfriend and we cried together over the phone. I had no idea how long it would be before I would see him again. We just held the phone to our ears for a while listening to the silence. Neither one of us wanted to say good-bye...

My eyes glanced over my bedroom once more as I stood in the doorway and leaned against it for support. I scanned over the list of things to pack I was holding in front of me in my trembling hands. My wardrobe consisted of a few dresses and several summer blouses that were suitable for everyday wear.

My fall jacket and winter coat hung next to a fitted suit, and then there was a row of empty hangers. My dresser drawers were almost as empty. I looked over my inventory of clothes and back at the list in my hand. I had only a few of the items on my list, and not enough time to shop for those I didn't have. So I scavenged through my skimpy wardrobe of clothing and packed what I could into my suitcase.

Within a few hours I was in the car on my way to the airport, to board my flight to Basic Training in Alabama. I did not know it at the time, but I would be coming back to Alabama to attend Collage there in the future. But for now it was to be my new home away from home, and I had an uneasy sense of foreboding in my mind.

My first experience on an airplane was surprisingly pretty safe. I boarded the plane leaving for Chicago and settled into a window seat near the middle of the plane. I was a little excited, but nervous about what to expect. The fasten seat belt sign went on and the pilot's voice came over the speaker. A stewardess held a sign up in front of her and began to give some instructions, and we were on our way.

After a while the sign to unfasten seatbelts came on. I was served a lunch that consisted of food I was not familiar with. There was a salad that had some fat worm- like things in it. I was afraid to eat it. Years later I learned the worm-like things were shrimp.

The Little crate-like plane I boarded later in the day, took me onto the Base in Alabama. Without a doubt it was truly scary! I felt my ears stop up as it began to lift up higher and higher into the grey dusky evening sky. It must have been the middle of the night when we arrived in Alabama. I felt the prickling chilly night air as we stepped off the plane. I had not dressed nearly warm enough.

I began to tremble as I wrapped my skimpy short sleeve sweater around my body. The others were talking loud and laughing as we one by one huddled together on the grey chilly cement landing strip pavement in front of us. I don't know what all the chatter was about, I hardly felt like talking myself.

Suddenly without warning, in front of us I heard this loud angry voice, belting out expletives at us to shut up and move out. I thought, that meant that we should move toward the big wood structure in front of us. I was right. We began to shuffle along and again the voice belted out, pick up your feet and more expletives.

Inside we were huddled together like sheep waiting for the slaughter. We were separated and then taken in smaller groups to our sleeping quarters. There we were assigned beds. I remember thinking to myself, what the heck have I gotten myself into? My bed at home seemed like a bed in a five-star hotel compared to the bed I was assigned to sleep in. To make matters worse, we were told that we had to be up within just a few hours to begin our day. At that time we would be briefed on our schedule and regulations as new recruits.

I recall getting very little sleep that night and winking to God before falling off to sleep. That is how sleepy I was and describes how short my prayer to God was. It was not at all a conversation prayer, but one of those canned prayers we learn from our parents or at church. They have been repeated again and again, hundreds of times. Well this one we usually say before we go to sleep at night. You know the one. Now I lay me down to sleep I pray the Lord my soul to keep. If I should die before I wake, I pray the Lord my soul to take. What was different about it this time is that it was not just a rote prayer I had memorized. I actually wanted to reach heaven and sense that God was seriously listening to me this time.

I wish I could say that my prayer life while in the military was some great ebullient connection with God. But it wasn't. It was more like moments of quiet desperation and at times an utter expression of my neediness as a sinner who has simply lost her way.

God didn't seem to so much care about how skimpy my prayers were. He didn't even care so much about the times I did not pray at all. It was like I was always on God's radar. And He would always show up, just when I needed Him the most. And Just like He does all of His lost sheep, God cared lovingly and tenderly for me…

WEEKLY PRAYER BITES: A SOLDIER'S SALUTE TO PRAYER

Day1. Ghost Buster: Do you believe in ghosts?

Day2. Sex 102: Were you sexually active as a teenager?

Day3. Family Matters: How did you get along your parents as a teen?

Day4. Back to the Future: What were your plans for after high school?

Day5. Encountering God: When was your very first encounter with God?

Chapter 2

PRAYER AT THE FAMILY ALTER

My prayer life did not really began to take shape and become intense and with purpose until I became a wife and mother for the very first time. Not necessarily in that order. Military life for me was not kind. I did a lot of things wrong and a lot of wrong things were done to me. I did not take my experience like a trooper. But one thing I learned from the military that has stayed with me is self-discipline.

I learned also to take whatever hand life deals me and to make the best of it. I was pregnant and a single woman at the time of my discharge from the military. I need to take a time out to say this. We may make wrong decisions and get messed up in the process or we might go down the wrong path in life, yet God does not give up on us.

God sees the best in us still. And God does not change His mind about us. The good work that God begins in us, He will finish if we let Him. It does not matter how bad it looks or how far we have strayed from God, it is never, never, never, too late to turn back to God. God is rich in mercy for His mercy endures forever!!

I became pregnant for the very first time while on active duty in the military. The year was 1965. I was stationed in Maryland at the time and worked at WRAMC (Walter Reed Army Medical Center), as a Medical Corpsman Specialist. The father of my unborn son was an Army veteran suffering from PTSD (Post-traumatic Stress disorder).

At that time I had no clue that I too would years later be diagnosed with the same disorder. I will call him Art for the sake of keeping his name anonymous. Art was a very manipulative and controlling man with a pre-disposition toward violence. My behavior was not admirable at the time either. You may not have served in the military, but maybe you can identify with what I am about to share with you.

I was driven by my corrupt sensual nature, obeying the impulses of the flesh and impure thoughts in my mind. I was an easy prey in my sinful fallen state. I had no idea of the danger I was in, so while I was wallowing in foolish naivety, Art was able to lure me into his web of secrets and calculating lies.

After getting me pregnant, Art, one day in a jealous fit of rage beat me and viciously raped me at gun point! I survived that ordeal, but the emotional fall-out from it left me emotionally scarred for a very long time. After that horrific experience I vowed to never put myself in a life-threatening situation ever again at the hands of a man. So I began to erect this wall around me and to suppress those painfully damaging memories. My trust in human beings had eroded, but my trust in God took on a greater significance.

After my first son was born I hid myself in the rudiments of Christianity. I re-connected with my church family and became an active member serving as an usher and singing in the church choir. I felt I had messed up my life enough and now I needed to make amends for all of my misdeeds.

My goal was to be this authentic pure Christian woman. I was certain God would be pleased with me if I tried harder to be good and did what He required of me. I went through this charlatan phase in my Christian walk for some years before I understood that being a Christian is not about me, or a to do list that I followed daily, but about God and what He can do in my life. And being a Christian is about what Jesus did for me on Calvary and accepting Jesus into my heart sincerely.

It's something about being a wife or parent that sometimes brings you to your knees. The responsibility that goes with either can be overwhelming. It wasn't until after one failed marriage and another headed for failure that I realized I couldn't do it all and be all things to everyone who needs me. I learned that while I can't be that super woman others want me to be, God can be all that and more.

I learned to call on God and to depend upon Him to meet my needs. I referred those who had unmet needs to God much of the time once I figured that truth out. And even when I can't hear what God is saying all the time, and don't feel Him with me, I learned that God is always there. One minister explained it this way. God is at work the minute we pray working out kingdom business in our behalf in order to bring about the very best possible result to our situation or request. God is not using power to get things done, He is that Power!

If you can identify with what I'm saying give yourself a high-five! How reassuring and comforting it is to understand just how powerful God is! Even more awesome is to understand that we created finite beings can tap into God's power. It all boils down to the heart. It's a heartfelt interaction with the sovereign God of the universe, being present with Him one on one.

I was sick a lot after my military service. I was a chain smoker back then as well. I picked up the habit while in the military. It was so bad that I would find butts and empty the old tobacco out and roll my own when I had no money to buy a pack. One time I ran out of cigarettes and asked my husband to buy me a pack. He told me we needed bread too and he didn't have enough money to buy both. I told him to get the cigarettes or else... It was just that bad.

Part of my sickness was because of diseased kidneys. In my mid-twenties I was diagnosed with Polycystic Kidney Disease. I suffered with female concerns too following a miscarriage. I had the miscarriage several months after my first son was born. My body was not ready to carry another pregnancy so soon. Another reason was due to the fact I was on the pill and should have delayed sex for a while before trying to get pregnant again. My husband knew that my first born son was not his biological child. So naturally he began hounding me to have his biological child.

He was willing to marry me and raise my first born as his but not willing to wait patiently for his own biological child. I had no idea just how long the wait would be for my husband. It turned out to be years instead of the anticipated months before I would conceive another child and carry the pregnancy to full term. It was eight years to be exact. I can empathize with women who are barren because of those years of failing efforts to conceive. I was so miserable and desperate.

My husband was relentless in his request for me to conceive his own biological child to the point of making me feel unloved and unappreciated much of those years. Each month I dreaded the thought of wondering if I was pregnant or not. I couldn't bear to look at pregnant women or newborns, or children with their mothers. I went to numerous doctors and clinics without success. I went to pastors requesting prayer for me, hoping by some miracle I would conceive.

My last ditch effort was my plea to a friend of mine who was making a pilgrimage to a Holy Shrine to take my prayer request with her to place it on the shrine platform. It didn't matter at that time to whom or what God she was praying to. I was desperate to conceive a child for my husband by hook or crook. I know now how foolish it was for me to think that way. While there is only one true God eternal in heaven, everyone does not believe the same way.

She agreed to do it and not long after that I finally conceived again! It should have been a happy time and experience for me but it was anything but that. Shortly after I announced I was pregnant my husband started acting strange. I learned he was having an affair. He announced that he did not want a child at the time and he really didn't want to be married. He didn't want a divorce, just a legal separation so he could continue his affair.

To my shock he also suggested I get an abortion! I couldn't believe my ears. Get an abortion! I decided that was out of the question and continued the pregnancy without much encouragement or support from my husband. I was a basket case much of the time and had to take meds to get to sleep and for the depression I just could not shake. I actually hated myself. My health in general was affected by the whole situation I found myself in month after month and day after day.

Finally my second son was born. It's crazy how when he was lifted up for me to see right after giving birth, he actually looked the way I had felt during that pregnancy. His hair was standing straight up on his head and his little frame seemed twisted and distressed. I learned some many years later that he had been scarred in other ways as well.

He was born with a mental illness that manifested itself when he was a teenager. But I was actually adding to my poor health condition during that pregnancy also by smoking cigarettes. If you have never smoked please don't start. By the time my second son was born, I had a pack and a half a day cigarette smoking habit. I smoked a menthol brand. It was both the nicotine and menthol that I became addicted to.

It finally came to a head one day when I was alone standing in our kitchen. I felt so sick to the stomach. I was tired of feeling that way day in and day out. I cried out to God in utter desperation; God help me!! Something happened on the inside that day which I had never experienced. God saved me!! The Greek word translation for the English word "save" is "sozo". In the Lexicon "sozo... means: preserve or rescue from natural dangers and afflictions...save from death...bring out safely from a situation fraught with mortal danger...save from disease...from demonic possession...be restored to health, get well...keep, preserve in good condition...thrive, prosper, get on well...save or preserve from eternal death..."

I was compelled by the voice of God that day to take the remainder of the pack of cigarettes I held in my hands and throw them in the trash. I obeyed the voice of God and was instantly, miraculously healed from my cigarette addiction. I never craved or picked up another cigarette from that day forward. Whenever I have the opportunity, I share this story of God's divine intervention in my life. Every now and then He reminds me of His power to save when I forget and try to do things in my own power.

At one time there were four sons in my care under one roof. The year was 1981. I was in my second marriage during that time. I belonged to a Bible teaching church. Not only was the Bible being taught, how to apply biblical principles to everyday life was also taught. It was during this time that I learned about the "Family Alter". At first I thought it was a physical man-made structure.

You might be thinking that same thing. Let me tell you that is far from the truth. The Alter was an experiential prayer concept shared with family members at an arranged time and place. A form of corporate prayer and worship to God is expressed during this time. Yet each individual has opportunity to participate in their own unique way.

So my sons and I came together every morning and evening to the Family Alter to share and draw close to one another and God.

This Family Alter lasted for many years, until the boys were on different schedules and out of my household. I have fond memories of those days. I believe that somehow that Family Alter helped to shape our characters and strengthen our resolve for the storms that we each would face in the years ahead. If you want to engage in something rich in your family experience, I invite you to begin your own Family Alter. You'll be glad you did...

WEEKLY PRAYER BITES: PRAYER AT THE FAMILY ALTER

Day1. The Rabbit Died: What was your first pregnancy like?

Day2. My Baby Daddy: What kind of person is the father of your child/children?

Day3. WWGD (What would God do?): Do you know what God requires?

Day4. The Choice: What is your opinion about Abortion?

Day5. Family Matters: What is one tradition your family has?

Chapter 3

PRAYER IN THE PURSUIT OF HIGHER LEARNING

Prior to entering a four year school of higher learning I completed a Vocational Training program at a two year community college in my home town. The year was 1977. I had just been diagnosed with a terminal illness several years prior to enrollment. I remember the struggles of being a single parent and battling my illness just to make it through. I was still active in church but not really experiencing much of God's power in my life. By God's grace I managed to complete my studies and finally walked across the platform to receive an "Associates Degree" in Business.

It was an evening ceremony. Some of my family was there to wish me well. I remember the sweat clinging to my body underneath my cap and gown. I felt a sense of relief and accomplishment that night, but I also felt that this was not the end of my story. It was actually the beginning of a long and tedious journey in the halls and class rooms of two campuses in two different states. I was blessed to be able to use the GI Bill to pay for my Community college courses. But the funding for my BA and Master's Degree would be available because of the mighty movement and the amazing operation of the grace of God.

I had pretty much settled into a routine after Graduating with my Associates degree. I had a job fairly soon at the same two year college I graduated from. I was a single parent still and dating the future father of my future youngest sons at the time. Although life was getting better for me financially I did not have very much material gain. I was renting a room from my older brother Roy and on the bus line to get to work and places I needed to get to. My credit worthiness was great at that time. In my mind I was living on top of the world. We have all been there at one time or another. Its' funny how, we forget about God so easily, when we are on top of the world.

I had come along ways from when I was eighteen without any tangible prospects for a future accept the Army. But what I failed to remember is that I did not get to where I was on my own. So I moved God aside and made decisions based upon whatever I thought I could do to make my life what I wanted it to be. The first thing I wanted was more children. So I had two more sons. Then I decided I wanted to buy a house for me and my four sons. So I bought a house. Things were working out for me pretty much how I wanted them to...

Reality did not set in until one day an Elder from the church I belonged to came by my house uninvited. My live in boyfriend was walking out of my bathroom in his undershirt just as the Elder, was about to get comfortable, on my couch. It was a scene similar to the woman caught in adultery. After being censored by my church, I married my live in boyfriend later that same year in a small ceremony.

That was one of the biggest mistakes I ever made! I had not married for love or money. I felt an overwhelming sense of pressure from my church to marry. Nevertheless there was something good that came out of that marriage. I learned that it is far better to listen to

God no matter what it feels like or looks like. God will be there with you no matter what. God still works in our messes.

My second marriage ended in a long separation and eventually divorce. It was during the long separation period that some mind altering and life changing events happened in my life. I began to experience a great time of soul-searching, and intense, consecrated prayers to God. It was a time when I was truly seeking after the heart of God.

At the time I was working a very good job with the government and meeting my mortgage and other financial and family responsibilities. But I discovered that I was not being fulfilled in my walk with God. For me the cup was only half full, because I had a compelling, insatiable desire to do full-time ministry for God. The well-organized plans I laid for myself in other areas, had not moved me one step closer to my spiritual fulfillment. It was when I let go and let God that things began to happen in a miraculous way for me.

Out of the ashes of a broken marriage and a fire that totaled my house, came the actualization of my heart's desire. My simple prayer that prior year before was simply; God use me! I think as I look back over the way God answered that simple prayer, I might have been more specific. It seemed like God had made a mistake in His answer. God answered in ways I could have never expected. I never anticipated that my marriage would get worse or that my house would be totaled by a fire. But while these events were negatives, they actually freed me up to make some new starts in my life.

My husband had supported me to an extent when I was doing ministry part-time, but when I shared my desire to do ministry full-time he opposed me every step of the way. My husband did not understand that it was God's plan for me to do full-time ministry. It was divine providence that rearranged things, and people and principalities to open the way for me to complete the educational requirements for formal full-time ministry.

I can attribute my spiritual growth during those years with being closely connected to God in prayer. I engaged in prayer the moment my feet set down on the campus of Oakwood College (Oakwood University). The year was 1988. I prayed about everything. There was a mix-up with my records when I tried to register. God fixed the problem so that I was not only able to register for classes I had advance placement status because of my previous college credits.

I needed a place for me and my three sons to live in. God provided a three bedroom house not far from campus. I needed a cash paying job on campus. God worked it out so that I worked in the cafeteria. I needed a car to get around in. God provided me with a car. Of course the enemy continued to attack me. I was disappointed that I was unable to enroll all three sons in Church School.

Even though a lot of things seemed to just fall into my lap, there was always something to keep me on my knees in prayer. I was seriously in continuous prayer mode as I matriculated through my studies at The Oak. The spiritual atmosphere on campus was electrifying!! I felt right at home with God there. It was not unusual for me to be in conversation with other students and suddenly we locked hands and prayed about something right then and there openly.

Not only was I under attack back then, my son William was a target as well. He was a troubled child most of his childhood. That seemed to escalate while I was attending Oakwood. William was a strong willed child as well. All my efforts to help him were met with resistance. We were constantly at odds with each other. I think I prayed more for William back then than I did for me and his other siblings. I share more about William in my book, "GOD I'LL TAKE THOSE CRUMBS", look for it in bookstores in the future.

If I had my way I would have graduated from the Oak, but God had other plans for me. In 1991 I transferred to Andrews University. My very first reaction when I stepped onto the campus was cultural shock!! All my life I had attended predominantly minority student enrollment schools. While Oakwood was diverse in its enrollment it too was a predominantly minority student body. The atmosphere was totally differently there for me.

At Andrews I felt the pressures of the University level academia right away. It may be in part because Andrews had University level accreditation that I felt the expectations were much higher and more demanding there.

I was doing fairly well at Oakwood academically, but I was sure God was expecting too much from me this time by leading me to Andrews University. I had avoided the heavy weight courses while I was at Oakwood. Greek was one of those courses. Most of the

Religion students at Oakwood dreaded this particular class because of the reputation of the professor who taught it at Oakwood.

I wasn't going to break the mold by serving myself up as a sacrificial lamb by taking a Greek class at Oakwood. I believe God understood this fear in my mind. So he re-arranged people, places and principalities so I could take Greek without those fears. Not only did I enroll into the Greek class at Andrews, I took this class during the Summer Enrollment session. Believe me I know this had to be a God thing. To my surprise and delight I really enjoyed studying Greek. I passed Greek that summer with an "A" grade!! That is just an example of the numerous ways in which God met me there at Andrews and supplied all of my needs.

The electrifying spiritual atmosphere wasn't happening there for me at Andrews, but God was there to make up the difference. Small prayer groups were available on campus and in the community that I could participate in. At times I hosted a small prayer group in my apartment. It was those focused groups and the concerted prayers to God that gave me just the boost I needed. Not only was I able to complete my undergraduate studies at Andrews University. God called me to come up a little higher. After completing a BA in Religion, God impressed me to enroll into the Seminary.

The assessment and evaluation test results required of students desiring to enroll into the Seminary suggested that I was not very suitable for the Seminary. It also concluded that I would likely experience a high level of stress and not be successful at completing my Masters of Divinity. I could bow out gracefully or I could trust

God. I chose to trust God, and I am glad I did. Just as God had done so many times in my past, He showed up and showed out. There was never a need that I had during my Seminary experience that God did not supply. God was so good to me that I grew to love Him more and more.

I was praying with a friend of mine, Cecilia, one day. She opened her apartment to a group of us students each week to pray. She and I had been reading the word of God in Philippians 3:10(TELB) which says,

"[For my determined purpose is] that I may know Him [that I may progressively become more deeply and intimately acquainted with Him, perceiving and recognizing and understanding the wonders of His Person more strongly and more clearly], and that I may in that same way come to know the power out flowing from His resurrection [which it exerts over believers], and that I may so share His sufferings as to be continually transformed [in spirit into His likeness even] to His death,"

We both agreed that this is what we should ask God for. I was really more focused on the part about knowing God, in the power of His resurrection, not knowing the suffering of God. God answered that prayer in a way I never expected. God allowed me to know Him in the power of His resurrection, but also in the sharing of His suffering too. I have experienced the grief and suffering of losing not just one, but two sons.

If you have ever known the loss of a child, I believe that comes very close to the pain and grief God might have felt when He gave up his only Son Jesus for us. I now have the highest respect and love for God for His selfless act, and for Jesus giving up His life on a cruel cross for a sinner like me. If I had a thousand tongues I could never thank Him enough! There is really nothing more I can say to explain a God who sees our nakedness and sinfulness yet hears our every sincere prayer and answers them all. I don't know what your life looks like right now. Maybe you are going through something that has literally brought you to your knees. I encourage you to talk to God and to tell him all about it. What God has done for me he can do it for you. When I lost my two sons I could have cursed God and never prayed again. But God's love grabbed me out of a horrible pit and lifted me and healed my broken heart over and over again. There is no soul that God cannot save. And no sinner who can out sin God's matchless love.

My prayer life has evolved over the years. These days I operate in my call from God to be an Intercessor. I do not take this position lightly but soberly. In the last section of this book I will discuss this more.

WEEKLY PRAYER BITES: PRAYER IN THE PURSUIT OF HIGHER LEARNING

Day1. Out of the Ashes: Have you experienced a fire of any kind?

Day2. Education in 3-D: How many degrees have you completed?

Day3. Pay the Pieper: Are you in debt for your education?

Day4. Still I Rise: What personal tragedy have you overcome?

Day5. Prayer Can: Are you part of a Prayer group?

Chapter 4

PRAYER IN THE SHADOWS OF DEATH

My classes were almost over and in a few short weeks I would be graduating the Seminary; the year was 1996. I was so happy that I was near the end. But I still had not completed the required Basic CPE (Clinical Pastoral education) training for students who planned to become a Chaplain. The basic CPE could be completed at any time during the Graduate program. But it was usually done during the summer months.

It was very difficult for me to do my CPE at any time because I had my sons with me and also I would have to quit my paying job to do it and I needed the money to provide for me and my sons. I was almost ready to give up when God stepped in again to rearrange people places and principalities just for me. A recruiter from Colorado, who was over the Chaplain training program at Porter Adventist hospital, located in Denver Colorado, came to Andrews University. I did not even have to go anywhere out of Berrien Springs Michigan to interview for basic CPE! What I didn't know is the recruiter was actually interviewing for something bigger than that.

I was interviewed by the recruiter for a Chaplain Residency position that included a full year of CPE. Although I had not completed the basic CPE requirement, to my surprise after that interview, I was invited to be a part of the training program at Porter hospital. There were more qualified students than me who had been interviewed and they had already completed their basic CPE. But I was picked for the training out of all of them. You can't imagine how blessed I felt and humbled by it all.

Now I was faced with the problem of how I was going to finance the move. I began to save what I could and requested help from my church and friends so I could make the physical move from Berrien Springs Michigan all the way across the country to Denver Colorado. I now know that God has a sense of humor. Are you serious God?

By the time the day came for me to make the move I had everything I needed. I had never been to Colorado. My sons were Pathfinders at the time and ironically they had actually gone there for a big Pathfinder camping event the year before. It took place at the Red Rocks. They had come back from that experience so excited! After listening to their accounts of Colorado I had wondered what it would be like to live in a beautiful place like that; not knowing that one day I would see Colorado for myself and actually be living in Colorado.

I arrived in Denver Colorado in the month of September of 1996. A good friend of mine, who, was also at Andrews when I was there, was going to be in the same Training program at Porter hospital. She had done her basic CPE at Porter. Actually her family lives in Longmont Colorado. She had helped to arrange things so I could get a place to live in and with getting some of my basic needs met after I arrived in Denver.

Because I had not gone through the basic CPE I had no clue what to expect. The beauty of Denver and the mountains helped to settle my nerves. I had to depend upon my friend from Andrews and others to navigate Denver until I was blessed to get a car. But getting to my training at Porter was a piece of cake. I lived right across from Porter hospital. Could God have arranged things better? I don't think so. All of my needs and more were met that year.

It was easy to connect with a church family and to grow spiritually as well. The very nature of my training and the families under my care at the hospital kept me on my knees in prayer. At times all I could do to keep my sanity was to pray. I had never experienced so much death until now. It seemed like every day I was at the bedside of patients who were not expected to live or consoling the family of someone who had died. I was on call around every three days and I was often awakened in the middle of the night to be with a patient or a family.

At one point my CPE classes became very intense. I did not know it at the time but the training was supposed to get inside of my head. Until then I had kept most of my stuff to myself and suppressed the painful mess deep inside. I had no intention of allowing any of it to surface. In fact if I had known what CPE involved I might not have agreed to do it. But I had agreed to it so now I had to trust God that I would come out ok.

I got a few emotional bumps and scrapes from the fallout of my own stuff. But my prayer life became stronger as a result. I came to know the God of life much better and also the God of death more intimately. The training I received at Porter hospital was invaluable. I thank God for it.

I experienced a personal tragedy during that year that would stay with me for a very long time. My eldest son was almost killed in a motorcycle accident. I remember the events of that fateful day so well. I was going about my day as usual when I received a call from the young lady, who was a part of my son's life at the time. I listened as she told me what had happed to my son. Her words left me speechless and in a state of unbelief. My son had been seriously injured and was in the hospital in Indianapolis awaiting surgery.

Fortunately I was at home that evening when I got the call. I don't think I could have been much good for anyone that day if I had been at work. All I could think about was the fact that my son was in a serious life threatening condition and I was not there with him. In fact I had no idea as to how I could get to Indianapolis to be with him. I barely made ends meet on my modest stipend from Porter hospital. I slept very little that night.

The next morning I managed to pull myself together enough to show up at the hospital for my classes and on call schedule. As I sat at the table in the training room my heart began to twist up in tight little knots. My mind was cringing and swelling with pain and grief. When it was my turn to speak I just burst out in uncontrollable sobs. I wiped my eyes with my hands as the tears rolled down my cheek. With a trembling in my voice I shared what had happened.

Before I could finish talking one of the training staff interrupted me. He asked me how soon I could book a flight and told me not to worry about what the cost would be. The hospital took care of that. I couldn't believe how caring everyone was, and how God was doing it for me once again. He was rearranging people, places and principalities just for me so I could be in Indianapolis, at the bedside of my son.

I arrived at Methodist hospital in Indianapolis just in time to pray with my son before he went into surgery. The surgery went well but my son suffered a stroke while recovering from his injuries that left him paralyzed on his left side. I had my son back from the clutches of death but I knew in my heart of hearts that he would never be the same. I returned to Porter and completed my program while his father stayed in Indianapolis to help with our son's rehabilitation.

In the spring of 1997, near the end of the first year at Porter I requested a second year. But to my disappointment my recruiter had something different in mind for me that altered the course of events for me. His plans sent me into a tail spin spiritually. He declined my request. I couldn't believe that I was turned down. It wasn't just me he turned down however it was the whole group of us who had been invited to come to Porter that year.

But unlike the others I had no safety nets that were in place to keep me from crashing financially. The stipend from Porter hospital was my only source of income. I was suddenly in panic mode! How in the world was I going to provide for me and my sons now? I wish I could tell you that I was this invincible spiritual powerhouse to reckon with during the whole experience. Or that I was this spiritual giant who did not bend under the weight of adversity. But I was none of these.

I became a total wreck. I went into a deep depression and became angry with God and everyone I felt was responsible for me being in Colorado. I wrote my brother in Indianapolis a rather morbid letter, expressing to him I had nothing left to live for. I was not planning to end my life I just wanted to let him know just how miserable I was. My landlord was threatening to put me and my sons out on the street because I had no money to even pay the rent.

I felt like a complete failure. My friends were a real blessing to me at that time they helped out as much as they could. My pastor at that time went to bat for me with my landlord so that I was not actually evicted from my apartment. And my brother sent me money to pay at least one month of my back rent in order to prevent me from being evicted as well.

During this time I was still praying but it seemed like God was asleep and He wasn't answering my prayers. I sent out my resume to other Hospitals and even to Prisons trying to get hired but nothing I did to get hired or a second year of CPE materialized. Finally when I had prayed all I could pray and did all I knew to do I told God I was about to lose my mind if He didn't do something. That's when God blessed me. He once again rearranged people, places and principalities just for me. I got an unexpected call from an administrator over a Community Corrections facility in Littleton Colorado, to come in for an interview. It had been months ago that I had sent them my resume and I had forgotten that I had even applied for a position there. The very day I went in for my interview I got the job! I knew it had to be a God thing.

The man who hired me had actually been looking for several months for someone with my spiritual background to complete his team of staff workers. Somehow my resume had been buried under a pile of papers on his desk all that time and he had only come across it the very day he called me to come in for an interview.

It was not a second year of CPE and it wasn't a Chaplain position in a hospital or Prison, but I truly believe it was where God wanted me for the time being. I loved that job and it kept me financially solvent so I could provide for me and my sons at least for a while. There were also other benefits. While I worked at Community Corrections I was able to provide a spiritual presence for the men and women who lived there and were transitioning back into the community.

Although I was there to minister to them, quite often I actually learned some very interesting and valuable lessons from some of them about life, God and my faith. I learned to be grateful for what I have and to never ever take my personal freedom for granted. Except for the grace of God there go I!!

WEEKLY PRAYER BITES:

PRAYER IN THE SHADOWS OF DEATH

Day1. Almost There: How close are you to your goals?

Day2. What daily practices could get you closer to your goals?

Day3. One From Among Many: Are you unique?

Day4: All of That and So Much More: Are you financially stable?

Day5. Caring For Others: Are you a caregiver?

Chapter 5

PRAYER IN THE MISSION FIELD

How I ended up half way across the world in South Korea (Land of the Morning Calm) is another one of those God things. Someone once said, "When you're down to nothing, God is up to something." It was like that for me just prior to me going to South Korea. And yes it is really true that God works in mysterious ways.

After working as a counselor for Community Corrections for about a year I was employed as a Para- Teacher at an Elementary school. Again, neither of these jobs was within my field of study even. But both were so gratifying and I truly loved what I was doing. Even so neither job lasted beyond a year for some strange reason. I am quite sure God knows why, He just didn't shared that information with me.

Near the end of my teaching contract I was contemplating whether or not to do another year there at the school or look for something in my vocation. During that time I got a call from a longtime friend to come to Michigan to possibly fill a position with a Women's Shelter. I had worked for this particular shelter while I was studying in the Seminary at Andrews University.

The offer was for the position of "Director" of the facility. I had the required degree, background and experience for the position. I felt truly honored to even be considered for such a great position!! It didn't matter to me that it was not a chaplain position. I had a phone

54

interview with the current Director and was formally offered the position. I made arrangements with my Landlord in Denver to get out of my lease and made the physical move to Michigan.

The current Director, who was still there when I arrived in Michigan, would be leaving soon to assume a position in the state of Washington within a few months. The plan was for me to work temporarily as an Administrative Secretary at the Shelter until then and move immediately into her position once she left. I was happy that the secretary position would only be temporary. I was not a fast typist at all and really had no background training for that type of work. But I determined that I would do the best I could to make the best of an awkward situation.

To my dismay and great disappointment the move to the Director position never happened. I discovered that the Board of Directors for the Shelter preferred a couple to fill the opening rather than an individual. So I remained in the temporary position longer than I had hoped. To make matters worse the person that they hired to work on site as the director had basically the same education I had accept I had an additional year beyond Graduate school of Clinical Pastoral Education. But his spouse was a Psychology major working on her Doctorate. There was really no way that I could compete with that.

The new Director and I did not work well together at all. Both of us were generals in a sense and we bumped heads often. It got so bad that one day he called me into his office and suggested that I quit my position there at the shelter. To me that was an insult because although I was not the best secretary I pulled my weight and did my work. It was simply not to his satisfaction. The other problem was that I was not a quitter. The jury is still out as to whether or not that was a good thing.

I recall that while I was a student at Oakwood College (Now Oakwood University), I had enrolled in a Black Studies class that was so way over my head. According to the powers that be at Oakwood I happened to be classified as a "non- traditional" student, which was really an "older student". I was even a member of "OOSA" (Oakwood Older Student Association). I graduated High School in 1963, so I had been out of school for quite some time before returning to study towards my undergraduate and graduate degrees.

During my Elementary and High School days, Black history was not a part of the curriculum and so it was not being taught back then. And it never was taught as rigorously as it is now. Although the class was very interesting there was just too much information for me to assimilate within the short time frame that I had to work with. By the time it was mid-term I was just blown out of the water. My test scores and grades in that class at that time was mostly in the low "D" and "F" ranges.

Another woman who was around my age was struggling in that class too but she had sense enough to drop the class. Not me; I just dug my heels in harder and determined to pass the class. The saying that pride goes before a fall is really true. I passed the class but my Grade was a "D-minus". I may have won the battle but I lost the war. My grade point average took a blow to it and less than half of what I had studied so hard to learn was retained in my mind.

After my boss at the Women's Shelter suggested that I should quit I began to do some soul searching to determine why was I still there at all. It seemed like I was between a rock and a hard place. Here I was away from family, the closest family lived roughly around two hundred miles away. That would include an older brother Roy, and my oldest son James and a host of other family in Indianapolis. But if my move to Michigan was really a "God thing" what was God saying to me in all of this? And why did I experience all of the struggles I was having at the Shelter? I prayed about it but I did not have an answer right away.

The move did make sense in a way because it give me an opportunity to spend more time with my eldest son James, who was still recovering from his motorcycle accident. I made the two hundred mile trip to Indianapolis just about every other week-end just to spend quality time doing fun things with him. For that reason alone living and working in Michigan and being closer to Indianapolis was priceless! I was having so much fun that it never even occurred to me that my trips to Indianapolis was going to someday come to an end.

After struggling for almost a year to keep my job at the Shelter I was finally fired. That was at the top of the list of things that have embarrassed me. In fact I was sure it was the worst thing that could ever happen to me at the time. I had never ever been fired before. What made it so bad is that I was also ill at the time. Two weeks prior to being fired I had been diagnosed with a hernia that had become seriously perforated and required surgery. It looked like there was no way out of these dilemmas for me.

I did what most of us do in our messes. Instead of trusting God I began to worry and I had an extended pity party for myself. God could have left me in that state of mind but I am so glad He didn't. While I was still in my stuff and complaining, God was busy rearranging people, places and principalities again just for me. The good news was that I could get the surgery at a VA hospital at little or no cost to me because I am a Veteran. And since I was fired from my job, I had more than enough time to recoup from the surgery.

Because I was fired I was sure I would not even qualify for unemployment benefits. To my surprise being fired actually worked in my favor in a way. Because I had not actually received training for the Administrative Secretary position I was fired from, I was able to collect unemployment. And through the encouragement of my Pastor, family and friends I began to focus on living again. But it was God who took me in His arms and so lovingly carried me through my personal storms that were raging in my life at the time.

There were more health issues too that seemed to pop up out of nowhere during that time of being still as well. I began to lose a lot of weight very quickly. I had very little energy even though I got at least eight hours of sleep. A size eight dress size was actually hanging off of me. I had a chronic cough and my chest hurt much of the time. I went to the doctor after this condition seemed to linger on for several months. I was given a possible diagnosis at the time for "Sarcoidosis", which is a disease that attacks the immune system. I had never even heard of this disease before. The doctors wanted to do a lung biopsy to confirm what they suspected. But I was in no mood to have more invasive procedures done at that time. So I bought some over the counter vitamins and pain medicine and decided to live with whatever medical condition I had at that time.

Aside from my health issues I still was faced with the fact that I needed a job. My unemployment was about to run out soon and I had no clue as to what I was going to do. I knew that to work as a Chaplain would be too stressful and physically draining on me at that time. I barely had enough energy to get me through the day let alone work a job. I was almost ready to throw in the towel and give up when something happened that would change my world forever.

In my mind I was running out of options. I had done all that I could do. I had gone as far as I could go. I had more than enough education. An Associate degree in Business, a Bachelor's degree in Religion with a Minor in Behavioral Science, a Masters of Divinity and a year of Clinical Pastoral Education. But none of that mattered at the moment. I was in a poor state of health and no amount of education could change that fact.

In only a few months, I would be without an income to sustain me. At that point I would be unable to make my car payments and pay my rent. It was then that I realized that I had no place else to go except to God. I felt like the Prodigal son in a faraway land, who finally realized that he did not have to wallow in the mire and mud, because his father was rich in houses and land. With his father there were benefits that he was still entitled to.

I thought I had come to Michigan to be the Director of a Women's Shelter. But just as God instructed Elijah to hide himself by the Brook Cherith, I later in retrospect realized that I too was set up by God so He could bless me and use me to build up His kingdom in a strange land. But in order to get me ready for my next assignment, like He did Elijah, God had to first humble me and cut me down to size. I was right where God wanted me. And God knew exactly what he had in mind for me. There has never been a time that God did not know what was best for me.

God always has a plan, and He never runs out of power. There is never a time that God is not being God. And there is nothing too hard for God. If God said it He can perform it. In Jeremiah 1:12 (TELB) it says, *"Then said the Lord to me, you have seen well, for I am alert and active, watching over My word to perform it."*

So I settled into a time of resting in God and waiting on God to perform His word.

Pastor Bedney was pastoring during that time at the Niles Philadelphia church in Niles, Michigan. He began mentoring me, and he allowed me to use my ministry gifts in that church. Also, during that time I went on campus to the library a lot and began to read and study my Bible more. On one of my trips to the library I ran across a campus newsletter and began to read it. That is when an advertisement for Missionary work in South Korea caught my eye. I couldn't wait to get back to my apartment to read it more carefully.

The advertisement said that The SDA English Institute in South Korea was looking for Volunteer Missionaries to teach English as a second language. In exchange for a year of teaching they would provide housing and a monthly stipend and pay for the trip over there and back to the States. There was a phone number and a name of a contact person to get the process going. I was so excited I could hardly sit still. My mind was racing. I was well qualified to teach and it wouldn't be too stressful or draining on my health either. It was a perfect solution for me! I was getting ready to call the number but realized it was Sunday. I thought I might as well wait until the next day. No one would be there to answer my call on a Sunday anyway. But I couldn't wait. I dialed the number and to my delight and surprise someone was there to answer the phone! The rest is history...

I convinced my doctor that I was well enough to make the trip and teach for a year in South Korea. I thought about the very first time I left home to do a tour of duty in the Army. This time I would be leaving not only my family and friends, I would be leaving my country. For the first time in my life I would be a foreigner in a strange land. But it would be alright because it was a God thing and not my idea. So no matter what happened I knew that God was with me.

My faith in God was tested from the time I boarded the airplane to the time I stepped off the plane in Seoul South Korea. I was totally dependent upon God to keep me safe and well enough to keep up with the demands of my teaching assignment. There was always a real possibility that North Korea could decide to invade South Korea. I was living about forty miles from the boarder to North Korea. In spite of the risk involved I can honestly say that I felt safer there in South Korea than I did back in America.

The spiritual experience I had as a Missionary in South Korea was the best ever. I had wanted to do LE work, (Literature Evangelism) when I was at Oakwood but the timing was not right. While at Andrews I still had a compelling desire to love the world for Jesus, but again the timing was off. So here it is the year is 2002, some five years later when I am at my lowest state of existence ever, that I actually get to fulfill my desire to do missionary work.

I had so much freedom to do the things I love to do in South Korea. I gave personal Bible studies and led young and old people to Jesus. Every morning during the week I could select a scripture text and for three minutes expound upon it to my students. On Friday nights, I could participate or lead out in Praise and worship. On Sabbaths, I could attend church at the Institute and even preach if I wanted to. It was just a mountain top explosion of God's Spirit twenty-four hours a day for me. There were often times that God would impress me to just pray for everyone on the streets as I walked to the Institute each day. The streets were always crowded, so I expect to see hundreds of Asian people, whom I never met personally, that I prayed for who will be in heaven with me when I get there. One of the most endearing Bible studies was with two sisters. They were so excited and eager to learn about Jesus.

In the midst of all of the exuberance and euphoria, God must have had a conversation with Satan about me because I was attacked by Satan with such a deadly and vicious blow.

It was on a Sabbath morning that I received the news that back in the States my son William had died in a house fire. It was the way he died that brought me to my knees. He was knocked unconscious and sprinkled with a flammable substance and then intentionally set on fire. The Devil meant to take me out by breaking my Spirit.

He almost had me for a short while. But God wouldn't let me go. Because God had me wrapped up so tightly in His bosom no Devil in hell could have shaken me out. God had me wrapped up so good that I couldn't even hate the man who murdered my son. I had only compassion for him. In the depths of my pain and anguish God began to minister to me and guide me to scriptures and comfort me.

It was one scripture text that did more for me that any of the others God gave me. It was 2 Corinthians 5:1 (TELB),"*for we know that if the tent which is our earthly home is destroyed (dissolved) we have from God a building, a house not made with hands, eternal in the heavens*"...

I was still too broken however to make the trip back to the States to burry my son. My eldest son James and other family and friends took care of everything. It was the fact that my students needed me at the Institute that I was able to make it through the weeks and months that followed Williams' death. And eventually in time I was able to have some peace with it and return home to the States.

I didn't know how but I knew that somehow in God's providential care I would be able to go on living with the knowledge that my eldest son James had substantial disabilities from his accident and my with my grief over my son William's untimely death... It wouldn't be easy but it would be doable. I have learned how to truly lean on God in the days ahead.

WEEKLY PRAYER BITES: PRAYER IN THE MISSION FIELDS

Day1. The Big Picture: Is your life a Puzzle?

Day2. Expect The Unexpected: What happened this week unexpectedly?

Day3. Never Give Up: Are you a quitter?

Day4. A Balm In Gilead: Are you plagued with health Issues?

Day5. Strange Fire: Have you ever lived in a foreign country?

Chapter 6

PRAYER VISION

I believe in my ignorance of the fact, I was actually interceding for others long before I even knew anything about Intercessory Prayer. There was always something going on in my own family and with people I knew that simply called for divine intervention. So there has never been a time when I did not pray for others. The beautiful thing about Intercessory prayer and being called by God to intercede is the anointing of God upon your life.

The anointing is what breaks the yoke of the enemy. I have learned that through prayer for others my faith is renewed and charged. There are no limits or real boundaries that inhibit the prayers of an intercessor. Vast territories and whole countries and nations can be reached through intercessors. The greater our faith in God the more He entrust to intercessors. It is one of the most noble and unselfish gifts that God can bestow upon finite beings. Through the prayer of intercessors God comes shining through every time because only God can give the results and get the glory that is due Him.

So what is being an intercessor in technical terms? Zondervan's Compact Bible Dictionary describes Intercessory Prayer this way: "*Pe*tition on behalf of another; entreaty to God for their good and wellbeing." God is constantly searching the earth for those who are willing to be His conduits of prayer for others. He says in Ezek.22:30 (TELB), "*And I sought a man among them who should build up the* *wall and stand in the gap before me for the land that I should not destroy it, but I found none."*

Jesus Christ is the ultimate intercessor. Jesus Christ is our great High Priest in heaven interceding for you and me. He is now functioning as our representative, guaranteeing our access to the Father. So there is a method to follow in regard to intercession. We pray to God in the name of Jesus for others.

There is no question as to the importance of prayer. I like the way one writer puts it: "Prayer is the breath of the soul. No other means of grace can be substituted, and health of the soul be preserved. Prayer brings the heart into immediate contact with the wellspring of life, and strengthens the sinew and muscle to the religious experience..." Gospel workers, pp. 254,255

None of this is possible without being connected with God and Jesus Christ through the Holy Spirit. Without the Holy Spirit we are powerless to do anything meaningful. Romans 8:7 tells us, *"... the carnal mind is enmity against God..."* John 3:9 tells us, *"That which is born of the flesh is flesh; that which is born of the Spirit is spirit."* Too many people are under the false assumption that with the help of God the old nature, or the flesh, can be cleansed and purified. The truth is that the Christian life is not a modification or even an improvement of the old, but an actual transformation of nature. This is only brought about by the effectual working of the Holy Spirit.

So God gave me a vision of what a Spirit filled Prayer Ministry for individuals and the Church at large can be. This vision includes all of those who comprise the Prayer Ministry leadership positions of the church. Especially those in the position of responsibility in the church should feel a sense of love, duty, and consecration to God as intercessors. Christ is standing at the door of His church with His voice pleading for Intercessors, who will consecrate themselves to the work of God for the salvation of souls.

The church is the body of Jesus Christ. As such the church draws its life from Jesus Christ by way of the Holy Spirit and the authority of God's word the Bible. We are very near the end of the close of earth's harvest. God is releasing a special bestowal of Spiritual grace to prepare the church for the second coming of our Lord and Savior Jesus Christ. There a key elements, that should be at work operating in the church of God during this time.

The power of the Holy Spirit and the Spirit filled prayer of intercession. Paul tells us in Romans8:26 (TELB), *"So too the [Holy] Spirit comes to our aid and bears us up in our weakness; for we do not know what prayer to offer nor how to offer it worthily as we ought, but the Spirit Himself goes to meet our supplication and pleads in our behalf with unspeakable yearnings and groaning too deep for utterance."*

In light of the importance of this closing work in the church the Prayer Ministry should be well organized and well-oiled with the Holy Spirit. No stone should be left unturned in this great task. A Prayer ministry Flow chart that includes the following can be helpful:

- Prayer Ministry Coordinator
- Small group Prayer Cells
- Internal Affairs Prayer Leader

- External Affairs Prayer Leader
- Local Community Prayer leader
- Special interest Group Prayer Leader
- Youth Ministry Prayer Leader

Under each of these leadership positions would be a list of every conceivable area of concern for that particular department in the church. For example under the Local community Prayer Leader you might list the following:

- Local area churches
- Business community
- Municipal (Police, Fireman etc...
- Hospitals/clinics
- Judicial System
- Media (Radio, TV, Internet, etc...
- Social/cultural

As you can see the list can be very creative. Each area on the list would be under the leadership of a Small group cell leader.

I would be remiss if I did not address the concept of Fasting. The Bible is clear that some situations require both fasting and prayer. You can read the story in the book of Matthew chapter 17:19-21 where the disciples were trying to cast out demons without success and Jesus explained to them, *"But this kind does not go out except by prayer and fasting."*

In her book "The Difference Is Prayer", Ruthie Jacobsen says that, "Fasting is a primary means of restoration. Humbling yourself by Fasting releases the Holy Spirit to do His special work of revival in you. This changes your relationship with God and gives you a greater awareness of God's reality and presence in your life." I agree with her. I also believe that Fasting should be done reverently and soberly by the leading of the Holy Spirit. If you try to Fast on your own in the flesh you will run into problems. But if God leads you into a Fast He is responsible to bring you through it with success. There are different ways to Fast but I like the one found in the Bible in Isaiah 58:6, 7(TELB), which God approves of.

It says, *"[Rather] is not this the fast that I have chosen: to the bonds of wickedness, to undo the bands of the yoke, to let the oppressed go free, and that you break every [enslaving] yoke? Is it not to divide your bread with the hungry and bring the homeless poor into your house – when you see the naked, that you cover him, and that you hide not yourself from [the needs of] your own flesh and blood?*

Whether you are simply praying or doing a fast along with your prayer God is always calling us to communion with Him. I especially like the way one prolific writer says it, "If we keep the Lord ever before us, allowing our hearts to go out with thanksgiving and praise to Him, we shall have a continual freshness in our religious life…when this is in truth the experience of the Christian, there is seen in his simplicity a humility, meekness and lowliness of heart, that shows to all with whom he associates that he has been with Jesus and learned of him." COL pgs. 129,130

My friend however God is leading you to pray may I encourage you to get ready for the amazing, profound and prophetic outpouring of God's Holy Spirit in your life. What God has done for others He will also do it for you. As you partner with God as an Intercessor in your home, community and church you will reap amazing results!! God has promised it. Dare to believe…

Bibliography

Arndt, W.F. and Gingrich, F.W., edit, a Greek- English Lexicon of the New Testament and Other Early English literature (Chicago: University of Chicago Press, 1957).

Jacobsen, Ruthie. The Difference Is Prayer. Hagerstown, MD: Review and Herald Pub. Assn., 1998.

Sheets, Dutch. Intercessory Prayer, Ventura, Calif.: Regal Books, 1996.

White, Ellen G. Christ's Object Lessons. Washington, D.C.: Review and Harold Pub. Assn., 1941.

White, Ellen G. Gospel Workers. Washington, D.C.: Review and Herald Pub. Assn., 1941.

Wolkwitz, David. A Mighty Rushing Wind. Fallbrook, CA: Hart Research Center, 1999

Zondervan's Compact Bible Dictionary. Grand Rapids, MI: Zondervan, 1993.

www.ingramcontent.com/pod-product-compliance
Lightning Source LLC
LaVergne TN
LVHW091209080426
835509LV00006B/900